FOREWORD

The iconic Hadrian's Wall World Heritage Site runs over 130 miles from South Shields in the east and down the Cumbrian coast in the west. The museums along its line are managed by a number of different organisations, who came together to create, in 2017, a unique 'dispersed' exhibition across 10 sites, telling the story of Roman cavalry. This came from a desire to raise awareness of the full scale of the World Heritage Site and of the rich variety and high quality of museums and heritage attractions along its length, to explore the often overlooked presence of Roman cavalry troops on the frontier and to demonstrate that the museums along the World Heritage Site operate as an effective partnership.

We focused on Hadrian's cavalry in particular for two reasons, partly in honour of the builder of the Wall, but also because the two key texts for understanding the drill manoeuvres of the Roman cavalry, the *adlocutio* and Arrian's *Ars Tactica*, both date to Hadrian's reign. We also took a wider view of the cavalry throughout the Imperial Roman period.

The exhibition, and this publication, feature some of the finest surviving examples of Roman cavalry equipment from the Imperial period, a period when cavalry were very much a show element of an army that overall was very comfortable with providing spectacle, in an Empire that demanded it in so many aspects of life.

Bill Griffiths
Chair, Hadrian's Cavalry Project

© Ben Blackall

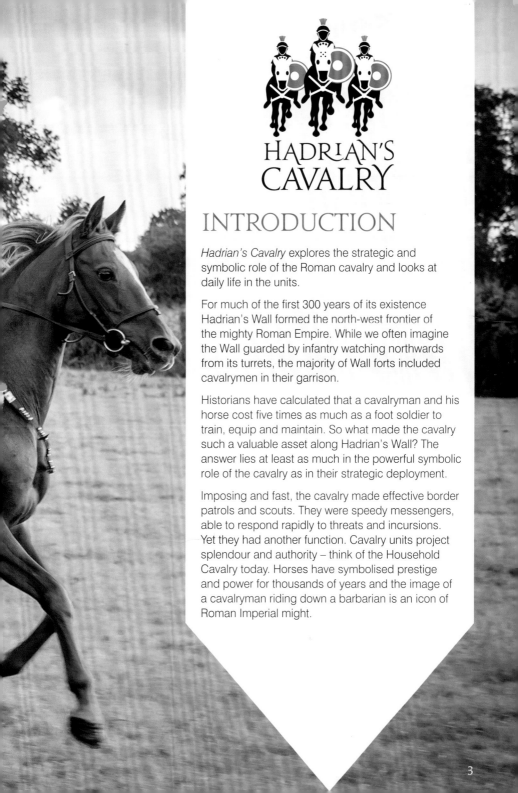

HADRIAN'S CAVALRY

INTRODUCTION

Hadrian's Cavalry explores the strategic and symbolic role of the Roman cavalry and looks at daily life in the units.

For much of the first 300 years of its existence Hadrian's Wall formed the north-west frontier of the mighty Roman Empire. While we often imagine the Wall guarded by infantry watching northwards from its turrets, the majority of Wall forts included cavalrymen in their garrison.

Historians have calculated that a cavalryman and his horse cost five times as much as a foot soldier to train, equip and maintain. So what made the cavalry such a valuable asset along Hadrian's Wall? The answer lies at least as much in the powerful symbolic role of the cavalry as in their strategic deployment.

Imposing and fast, the cavalry made effective border patrols and scouts. They were speedy messengers, able to respond rapidly to threats and incursions. Yet they had another function. Cavalry units project splendour and authority – think of the Household Cavalry today. Horses have symbolised prestige and power for thousands of years and the image of a cavalryman riding down a barbarian is an icon of Roman Imperial might.

THE
EVIDENCE

Opposite: A 3D scan of
the tombstone of Flavinus,
now displayed in Hexham
Abbey, shows a cavalryman
overcoming a cowering
barbarian.

© Newcastle University

Sources of Evidence

Our knowledge of the Roman cavalry comes from various sources of evidence. Our understanding changes as new information comes to light. So just how reliable is our evidence?

Written Evidence

Some Romans wrote about aspects of the cavalry, but for audiences who understood the subject. Scholars often disagree about details of translation of ancient texts.

ARRIAN

Born in Greece, Arrian was a Roman military commander, writer and friend of the Emperor Hadrian. Arrian's book *The Art of Tactics* (*Ars Tactica*) includes many details about the Roman cavalry and their equestrian displays.

HADRIAN'S ADLOCUTIO

An inscription from a parade ground in North Africa records Hadrian's speeches to troops. He comments on their manoeuvres, mixing praise with advice, and speaks directly to his soldiers, unit by unit. He tells the *ala I Pannoniorum*,

'you filled the training ground with your wheelings, you threw spears not ungracefully...'

Sculpture and Tombstones

Cavalry tombstones often depict a horse and rider and the equipment they used. But did the sculptors really know and understand what they were carving? And, because the carvings were intended to honour the dead, are the cavalrymen shown in their 'Sunday best' rather than regular uniform?

Opposite: This disc from Stanwix was probably used to label equipment with its owner's name. It reads: '[Property] of Gecus in the *turma* of Super'. *Turma* means troop.

© Tullie House Museum and Art Gallery Trust

Archaeology

Archaeology offers useful evidence, but artefacts are often found incomplete or without information about where they came from. This makes it difficult to understand what they are, and what they can tell us about the cavalry. Archaeologists try to match their finds with descriptions in written sources or details on sculptures.

Modern Reconstructions

Much valuable work has been done by people attempting to recreate Roman cavalry equipment as illustrations or full-scale replicas. Sometimes the process of reconstruction itself sheds new light on how an object was made and used.

All the Available Evidence

In reality we must use all the various sources to work out how the Roman cavalry operated, what their clothes and equipment looked like, and how that changed over the nearly 400 years that the Romans were in Britain.

Above: When experimental archaeologist Peter Connolly reconstructed a Roman saddle, he discovered that the shape gives riders a secure seat.

© Ben Blackall

Opposite: Excavating a fragment of discarded horse harness at South Shields. The decorative copper alloy studs are still in position.

© Tyne & Wear Archives & Museums

THE
ARMY

The Role of the Roman Cavalry

The mighty Roman cavalry striking terror into the heart of an unruly enemy attacking from north of the border. It's a popular image. But just how much fighting did the Roman cavalry do along Hadrian's Wall? Or was their real role something rather different?

Ancient accounts of the cavalry tend to be found in military histories or tactical manuals and therefore focus on battle scenarios. Yet the cavalry's role was also symbolic, projecting the power of Empire. For most of the Imperial period (the 1st to 5th centuries AD) the cavalrymen stationed on Hadrian's Wall and across the rest of the Empire rarely engaged in major military action.

Fast and highly mobile, cavalry troops made ideal border patrols, able to respond quickly to changing situations. For nearly 300 years, the Roman cavalry acted mainly as a police force, or even peacekeepers, along the Wall.

In battle, the cavalry often worked on the wings of a mainly infantry army. They drove off lightly armed skirmishers who could harass the infantry with javelins, arrows and slings. They were particularly useful against enemy foot soldiers, and many tombstones depict cavalrymen riding down defeated barbarians.

The Romans certainly controlled some territory north of Hadrian's Wall. Evidence from other frontiers demonstrates that the Romans taxed people north of their borders, and this may have been true in Britain too. Outpost forts such as Risingham and High Rochester north of the Wall housed mixed units of infantry and cavalry (*cohors equitata*) and units of scouts (*exploratores*), whose duties presumably included keeping an eye out for signs of unrest.

Above: Decorated shield boss. The upper inscription in Greek records its owner as Marcus Ulpius, a member of the Emperor Trajan's horse guard. The lower inscription probably represents the dedication of the boss to the memory of Marcus.

© UK Private Collection

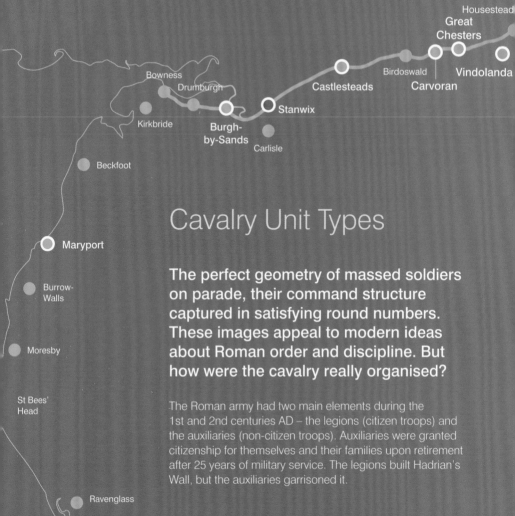

Cavalry Unit Types

The perfect geometry of massed soldiers on parade, their command structure captured in satisfying round numbers. These images appeal to modern ideas about Roman order and discipline. But how were the cavalry really organised?

The Roman army had two main elements during the 1st and 2nd centuries AD – the legions (citizen troops) and the auxiliaries (non-citizen troops). Auxiliaries were granted citizenship for themselves and their families upon retirement after 25 years of military service. The legions built Hadrian's Wall, but the auxiliaries garrisoned it.

Auxiliary Forces

Roman auxiliary forces (*auxilia*) had three core unit types.

Infantry (*cohors peditata*)

Mixed units of infantry and cavalry (*cohors equitata*)

Cavalry (*ala*)

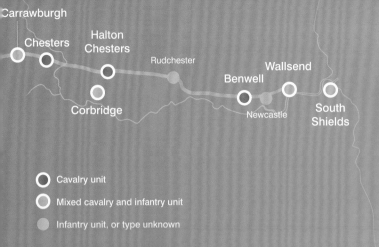

Carrawburgh
Chesters
Halton
Chesters
Rudchester
Wallsend
Benwell
Corbridge
Newcastle
South
Shields

○ Cavalry unit

◉ Mixed cavalry and infantry unit

● Infantry unit, or type unknown

Auxiliary units were nominally either 500 (*quingenaria*) or 1,000 (*milliaria*) strong. In fact, a mixed *quingenaria* unit was likely to have 480 infantry and 120 cavalry. However there is evidence that regiments were often below full strength. The cavalrymen who served in the pure cavalry units (*alae*) were higher status than those of the mixed units and were expected to be better horsemen.

Auxiliary Cavalry Units

Cavalry units (*alae*) were subdivided into troops (*turmae*) of approximately 30 riders per troop. The officer in charge of a troop was a decurion (*decurio*). The second in command was a *duplicarius* (literally – double pay), and the third in command a *sesquiplicarius* (pay and a half).

Special Units

Evidence from the 3rd century AD suggests there were irregular units in the Hadrian's Wall area, presumably including cavalry. The legions too had cavalry detachments. The Emperor and provincial governors had their own elite horse guards.

Cavalry Barracks

Three men to a room, their horses stabled within earshot,
within smelling distance, just the other side of the wall.
The cavalry barracks' design emphasised the intimacy
of horse and rider, and enabled their rapid deployment.

At Home with the Troop

Each auxiliary cavalry barracks housed the officers, men and horses of a troop (*turma*) in a single building. Trios of riders lived in the rooms at the back, their horses stabled in the adjoining front room. The decurion, his family and horses lived at one end of the building in a suite of rooms, including a stable.

The cavalrymen ate, slept and kept their weapons and armour, personal possessions and horses' harnesses in their rooms. Each room had a hearth for cooking and heating, set against the wall adjoining the stable. Grooms, slaves who assisted both men and horses, possibly slept in the space under the roof.

Keeping Clean

Stable floors were kept clean and dry to prevent hoof problems. Slaves replaced bedding straw or bracken every few days, and mucked out horse dung daily. The horses' urine drained into stone- or wood-covered pits and was probably neutralised with lime and left to soak away.

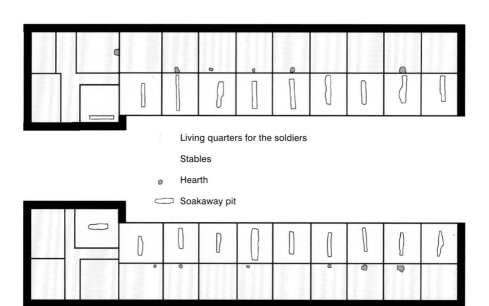

Living quarters for the soldiers

Stables

◉ Hearth

⬭ Soakaway pit

17

THE
RIDER

Opposite: Tombstone of Insus
of the *ala Augusta*. It is one
of a rider-type that depicts a
mounted cavalryman in action.
Found in Lancaster in 2005.

© Lancaster City Museum

19

Recruitment

Cavalrymen – made or born?
Did the Romans recruit locally or bring in specialist riders recruited abroad?

The Roman army recruited men from all over the Empire, a fact reflected in unit names. The Romans often recruited specialists, such as archers, from areas where those skills were developed young. They would be sent to specialist units, often far from their homelands. Whether the cavalry recruited specialist riders, we don't know. Possibly higher status pure cavalry units (*alae*) recruited young riders from areas where horse riding was part of everyday life, while mixed units (*cohors equitata*) recruited less experienced riders. Units based at the Wall may have recruited locals or the sons of serving soldiers from the area. Almost certainly, recruitment practices varied over time, and perhaps according to the status of a unit.

The *ala II Asturum* was formed in Asturias in Northern Spain, over 100 years before it was stationed at *Cilurnum* (Chesters) on Hadrian's Wall. A Roman gravestone from Gijon in Asturias records an otherwise unknown tribe, the *Cilurnigi*, in that region of Spain. The similarity between the name of the tribe and the name of the fort suggests that the unit maintained links to its Spanish homeland for more than a century. Did this include recruiting there?

Opposite: The Roman army recruited from all over the Empire. Areas in red show the countries of origin of the cavalry units who served around Hadrian's Wall.

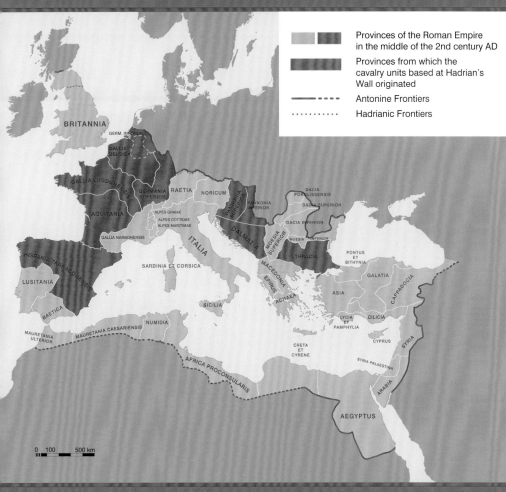

Provabili of the Roman Empire in the middle of the 2nd century AD

Provinces from which the cavalry units based at Hadrian's Wall originated

Antonine Frontiers

Hadrianic Frontiers

BRITANNIA

GERM. INFERIOR

GALLIA BELGICA

GALLIA LUGDUNENSIS

GERMANIA SUPERIOR

RAETIA

NORICUM

PANNONIA SUPERIOR

PANNONIA INFERIOR

DACIA POROLISSENSIS

DACIA SUPERIOR

AQUITANIA

ALPES GRAIAE

ALPES COTTIDAE

ALPES MARITIMAE

DALMATIA

DACIA INFERIOR

MOESIA SUPERIOR

MOESIA INFERIOR

GALLIA NARBONENSIS

ITALIA

THRACIA

PONTUS ET BITHYNIA

HISPANIA TARRACONENSIS

SARDINIA ET CORSICA

MACEDONIA

EPIRUS

ACHAEA

ASIA

GALATIA

CAPPADOCIA

LUSITANIA

BAETICA

SICILIA

LYCIA ET PAMPHYLIA

CILICIA

CYPRUS

SYRIA

MAURETANIA ULTERIOR

MAURETANIA CAESARIENSIS

NUMIDIA

CRETA ET CYRENE

SYRIA PALAESTINA

ARABIA

AFRICA PROCONSULARIS

AEGYPTUS

0   100   500 km

Training the Cavalry

Horse and rider working as one, disciplined and bold in the chaos of battle. Having mastered the basics, the cavalry practised and honed their skills in demanding training.

Cavalry horses were probably broken and trained by specialists before being assigned to specific cavalrymen. They were trained to overcome their instinct to flee when startled and to cope with the noise and excitement of battle. Trainers used long-reining to teach horses basic skills, as well as special steps, akin to modern dressage.

Horse and Rider as One

For the men, early training involved learning to control the horse while holding a spear in one hand, the reins and a shield in the other. Trainees progressed to combat skills – wielding sword and spear from horseback and throwing javelins accurately while riding at speed.

Training the Troop

With these skills in place, the trainees learned how to fight in a troop (*turma*). They learned to keep in line with other horses and turn all together as one. They learned special attack manoeuvres.

Some training took place within the fort, either out in the open or under cover in a purpose-built training hall. Other training took in all sorts of terrain to ensure that soldier and horse could deal with any conditions they met. They trained on level exercise ground outside the fort and on rough ground further afield. They learned to jump obstacles and cross rivers.

Training continued throughout the career of a cavalryman, who had to constantly maintain and develop his skills.

A Show of Force

Displays offered soldiers the chance to show off their skills and make an impression. The emphasis was on creating a spectacle and participants wore elaborate equipment and performed stylised routines.

Right: Replica of a bronze decorated cheekpiece from a cavalry helmet, dredged from the mouth of the Tyne, possibly from a Roman shipwreck.

© Tyne & Wear Archives & Museums

Opposite: Riders trained rigorously. As historian Edward Gibbon commented, 'They preserved peace by a constant preparation for war.'

© Ben Blackall

The Well-Equipped Rider

Cavalry display equipment was impressively
flashy. But in everyday duties, the cavalryman
and his horse offered rather a different picture.

Standard cavalry equipment included a helmet, body armour,
shield and weapons. The armour and weapons evolved as
the Romans learned from their enemies and adopted useful
equipment. Javelins became standard issue after the cavalry
encountered Numidians using them in the wars against Carthage.

Helmets

Helmet designs changed over time to offer ever better protection to the cavalryman. They covered the cavalryman's vulnerable skull, cheeks, ears and neck. Helmets with face-masks may have been worn only for displays.

Body Armour

Evidence from Roman sculpture, including Trajan's Column in Rome and cavalry tombstones, suggests that cavalrymen wore scale armour or mail rather than the overlapping strips worn by legionaries. Cavalrymen also wore leg protectors known as greaves.

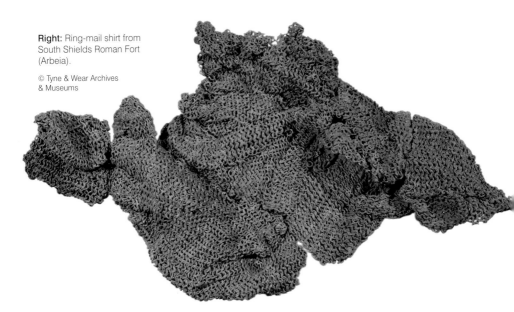

Shields

Images of cavalrymen show shields of various shapes, including rectangular ones with a curved top and bottom, oval and hexagonal ones. They were probably flat with a painted front. They had a metal rim and protruding central boss so riders could use them as weapons.

Weapons

A writing tablet from Carlisle gives an inventory of cavalry weapons. Each cavalryman had a sword, a fighting lance and two smaller javelins. Cavalry swords were longer than infantry swords, to make it easier for the mounted rider to reach an enemy on foot. Lances were handheld in combat. Javelins were thrown, allowing the cavalry to attack from a distance.

DIVINE PROTECTION

Soldiers commissioned craftsmen to decorate their armour with pictures and symbols they believed would protect them and bring them good luck. Mars, the god of war, was understandably popular. Other popular choices included Jupiter, the supreme god, the Medusa, who could turn people to stone, Gryphons, who guarded precious objects, and Hercules because of his strength.

Below: An iron and tinned bronze Butzbach type helmet. The decoration has a laurel crown, which suggests the wearer is celebrating victory. The other main decoration shows eagles, which were the symbol of Jupiter, king of the gods and patron of Rome and the Empire. It is late 2nd to early 3rd century AD.

© Musée d'Art Classique de Mougins (MACM)

The Cavalry and the Community

Soldiers, traders, farmers and their families dominated the Roman frontier in Britain.

Archaeological remains discovered at sites along Hadrian's Wall reveal the names of some individual cavalrymen from among those stationed in the area. The list below gives some examples.

Name	Rank	Evidence	Find site
Aelius Gemellus	Decurio (decurion, officer in charge of a troop)	Tombstone	Chesters
Anociticus Tineius Longus	Praefectus (commander of a cavalry unit)	Altar	Benwell
Aventinus	Curator (provisioned the troop)	Tombstone	Chesters
Flavinus	Signifer (standard bearer)	Tombstone	Corbridge, now in Hexham Abbey
Maelonius Secondus	Sesquiplicarius (third in command of troop)	Tombstone	Old Carlisle, near Wigton, Cumbria
Martinus	Decurio	Graffito	Birdoswald
Masclus	Decurio	Writing tablet	Vindolanda
Messorius Magnus	Duplicarius (second in command of troop)	Tombstone	Halton Chesters
Rufinus	Praefectus	Altar	Old Carlisle
Tagomas	Vexillarius (standard bearer)	Writing tablet and graffito	Vindolanda
Victor (a Moorish tribesman)	Calo (groom)	Tombstone	South Shields
Victor Venator (the Hunter)	Eques (horseman)	Writing tablet	Vindolanda

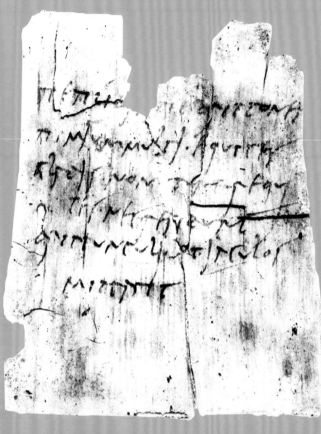

Relations With the Natives

A fragment of a wooden writing tablet gives us a glimpse of what the Batavians, a regiment at Vindolanda, thought of the native British cavalry.

'the *Brittones*, rather many of them cavalrymen, are naked. The cavalrymen do not use swords, nor do the *Brittunculi* mount to throw javelins.'

Here, 'naked' probably means without body armour. *Brittunculi* may be translated as 'little Brits' and is derogatory, suggesting 'nasty', 'pathetic' or 'wretched little Brits'.

© Ben Blackall

THE
HORSE

The Perfect Horse

'Well-bred members of the herd... step lighter than the others
and yet land their feet so daintily. The first and foremost will
lead the way to brave a river and the hazards of an unfamiliar
bridge. At the clamour of distant armour... he struggles to
contain his fiery breath in flaring nostrils. His hooves resound
as they eat up the ground and spit it out again.'

The poet Virgil, *Georgics*, book 3

The Romans recognised three classes of horse – noble, common and mule – with
mules essential as transport beasts of burden. Horse breeders improved bloodstock
by selecting and matching from among 50 or so breeds mentioned in Roman writings.

Breeders prized Celtic horses like those of the local auxiliaries from around Hadrian's
Wall. Cavalrymen liked Libyan and Spanish horses too, and a horse skull from *Trimontium*
(Newstead) in the Scottish borders is almost identical to a modern Arabian mare's.

Opposite: Local horse
breeds were well-adapted
to the local climate and
conditions.

© Ben Blackall

Right: Excavating a horse
skull at South Shields Roman
Fort (Arbeia).

© Tyne & Wear Archives
& Museums

The Well-Cared For Horse

**Daily grooming, massage and care.
Did cavalrymen look after their own
horses or get slaves to do it for them?**

Cavalry horses needed good care. Ancient authors
recommended daily grooming. We assume combs and
brushes were used, as today, but they rarely survive.
One writer proposed massaging a horse's legs and body.
Another advised rubbing down the horse's back by hand
to avoid hurting the horse with rough tools.

A cavalry horse ate about 12kg of feed a day, mainly grain
(oats or barley) and hay, supplemented with pulses and
legumes. Each cavalryman paid for his own horse's feed,
with payments deducted at source from his wages.

Resplendent Horses

**A comfortable odour of leather and horse
fills the cavalryman's nose as he polishes
his tack to a gleam. He mutters a prayer
as he cleans the embellishments, his ticket
to divine protection.**

Cavalry saddles, bridles and straps helped riders control
their horses. Specialist craftsmen made horse tack, whether
within the fort or in factories on the Continent. They sometimes
reused valuable elements in new kit.

Opposite: The engraving on
the central crescent *lunula*
of this horse's pectoral, or
breastplate, shows the gods
Hercules and Mercury.
There are geometric and
floral carvings, and two
ship's rudders below the
gods. The rudders are
symbols of good fortune and
offer amuletic protection.
This intricate pectoral dates
to around the middle of
the 1st century AD, and is
uniquely well preserved.

© Arachne –
Philipp Gross

Chamfrons are ceremonial head masks, similar to helmets. Highly decorative, they were made of leather, metal, or both. They covered the horse's forehead and some had perforated eye-guards.

Left: This is the most complete of nine chamfrons found at Vindolanda. It is made of cowhide with a goatskin lining. Most of the studded decorations have not survived or were removed to be reused.

© Vindolanda Trust

TO DECORATE AND PROTECT

Artisans travelled around military bases taking commissions to embellish cavalry equipment with pictures, graffiti and religious symbols for decoration and to invoke supernatural protection for the rider and horse. The richer the soldier, the more and better-quality decor he could afford.

Saddles and Straps

Cavalry saddles were leather-covered wooden frames with a raised 'horn' at each corner. The horns were stiffened with metal plates to give the rider a secure seat. Straps around the horse's breast and haunches and a girth around the belly kept the saddle in place. Decorative discs of metal or carved bone were often used where straps joined. Crescents, other pendants and beads were popular too.

Left: This stone relief from a temple shows the god of the universe, safety and success, Jupiter Dolichenus, riding a winged horse.

© English Heritage Trust

Below: Copper alloy brooch of a *hippocamp* facing to the right. Its body and fan-shaped fishtail were enamelled in blue and yellow.

© English Heritage Trust

Horses in Art and Myth

As winged beasts, straining chargers or hitched to a speeding chariot, horses were everywhere in Roman life.

Ancient Roman culture celebrated the beauty and strength of the horse. Horses played many roles in Roman mythology and ritual. In art and religion they were shown in realistic, symbolic and mythical ways.

Virtue, Status and Power

Workhorses provided vital transport and power in everyday life. A noble horse conveyed the status of its owner. Skilled horsemanship demonstrated the rider's Roman virtue in his strength, courage, intelligence and discipline in controlling the beast.

Mythological Horses

Many of Rome's divine and mythologised horses had their origins in ancient Greece, although their symbolism and appearance changed as Roman culture adopted and adapted Greek stories. Neptune's chariot was drawn by the *hippocamp*, a horse with a serpentine fishtail. Pegasus was one of a number of winged horses with divine origins and supernatural speed. Such winged beasts were associated with military heroism. They were symbols of immortality and are often found on funerary objects.

RITUAL
AND
DISPLAY

Opposite: Kalkriese type
helmet face-mask, dated to
around AD 0-40. This represents
the earliest face-mask type used
by the Roman cavalry. A similar
mask was found at the site of
the Battle of the Teutoburg Forest
in Northern Germany, fought
in AD 9.

Left: Bronze Ribchester-type helmet.

© UK Private Collection

The Power of the Mask

The masked soldier, inscrutable and austere, presented an uncannily imperturbable face.

Of all the cavalry armour it is the parade helmet with full face-mask that projects the indomitable power of Rome. A masked helmet protected the whole of the cavalryman's head. Yet perhaps even more important was the powerful effect of rendering men essentially 'expressionless', of transforming the man into his persona or role.

No one knows if an enemy ever witnessed these masks during military combat. One theory goes that the masks were ceremonial and worn only during the *Hippika Gymnasia* (equestrian games). The masks restrict peripheral vision, a serious problem in battle. Arrian, in his *Art of Tactics*, implies that face-mask helmets were only worn for displays.

Others believe that masked cavalrymen would have made such a fearsome impression they must have been used in war. They argue that the protection masks offered made up for the loss of peripheral vision and that their visual impact terrified opponents and lowered enemy morale.

The *Hippika Gymnasia*

Display cavalry charge into the arena, military standards aloft. Javelins fly. The crowd roars. It's an image we all know from films and books, but how accurate is it?

Below: The *Hippika Gymnasia*, by reconstruction artist Peter Connolly. In the foreground a rider adjusts his mask before mounting his horse. In the background a display team prepares to launch javelins at shield-bearing opponents.

© akg-images – Peter Connolly

Expert Horsemanship

A synchronised display of manoeuvres involved sections of the cavalry launching javelins at each other, first with one section stationary, then while both performed a circular ride. There were team games, then a roll call of the troops (*turmae*). After the roll call there were displays of individual skill and each soldier took three javelin shots at a target. Demonstrations of swordsmanship followed and cavalrymen in full armour mounted galloping horses.

How Do We Know?

Writing in the 2nd century AD, Arrian described the *Hippika Gymnasia* in his *Art of Tactics*. This type of display probably continued regularly for the next 200 years until the Emperor Diocletian (AD 294–305) completed his reform of the cavalry.

Arrian notes that Hadrian introduced new skills encountered in battle, such as Parthian-style mounted archery. Riders demonstrating newly adopted skills gave the appropriate war cry, for example a Celtic war cry to accompany Celtic manoeuvres.

According to Arrian, the highest ranking, most skilful riders entered the arena first, wearing full face-mask helmets. Like theatrical and gladiatorial masks, these signified that the horsemen were playing a role. Archaeologists have identified Amazon, Greek and Trojan character masks. This combination suggests that as part of the games cavalrymen may have re-enacted the myth of the foundation of Rome by survivors of the Trojan War.

Left to right:

Face-mask helmet showing a Trojan warrior.

The Crosby Garrett helmet, late 1st–2nd century AD (bronze), Roman / Private Collection / Photo © Christie's Images / Bridgeman Images

Face-mask of a Greek warrior.

© ALM BW – Limesmuseum Aalen

Face-mask of an Amazon warrior.

© ASM Munich

Epona, Goddess of the Horse

Epona is the perfect cavalry goddess. She is the Celtic divine protector of horses. The Romans adopted her cult from the Celtic horsemen they met and employed.

The Romans knew and employed the Celts as excellent mounted warriors. Riders helped keep the peace among tribes. They helped guarantee food security by protecting farmland. When Celtic riders joined the Roman auxiliary forces, they brought Epona's cult with them.

The Cult of Epona

Epona is usually depicted riding side-saddle or seated between horses, sometimes accompanied by a foal. Often she carries a cornucopia (horn of plenty) or basket of fruit, representing fertility. Sometimes she bears a *patera*, the small ritual vessel Romans used for making drink offerings to the gods.

Epona is the only Gaulish deity to have had a temple in Rome. Worshippers honoured her with an annual festival on 18 December. Celebrants decorated her image in their stables and temples with roses.

Epona's cult was accessible to ordinary auxiliary troops. It required no elaborate rituals, unlike the cult of the god Mithras. The cavalrymen could worship her alongside the *Campestres*, the Roman goddesses of the parade ground who offered protection to riders.

Opposite:
The goddess Epona. Many representations of Epona are found near the German Frontier and in France.

© Landesmuseum Württemberg, Peter Frankenstein und Hendrik Zwietasch

Right: Young cavalrymen far from home invoked Epona's protection over themselves and their horses.

© Ben Blackall

Epona in Britain

Two inscriptions to Epona are known in Britain. One at Carvoran on Hadrian's Wall, another at Auchendavy on the Antonine Wall. A small altar believed to have been dedicated to Epona was discovered at Netherby, near Carlisle, where there was an indoor riding hall used by the cavalry based there.

Acknowledgements

The main funder of Hadrian's Cavalry is the Arts Council England's Museum Resilience Fund

 Supported using public funding by **ARTS COUNCIL ENGLAND**

 HADRIAN'S WALL COUNTRY

 YEARS WORLD HERITAGE STATUS HADRIAN'S WALL

Project delivery partners:

 TYNE & WEAR archives & museums

 ENGLISH HERITAGE

 SENHOUSE ROMAN MUSEUM MARYPORT · CUMBRIA

 TULLIE HOUSE MUSEUM AND ART GALLERY CARLISLE

 VINDOLANDA CHARITABLE TRUST

 Northumberland National Park

Proud sponsors of *Hadrian's Cavalry*:

 CARLISLE CITY COUNCIL
www.carlisle.gov.uk

Christian Levett

Hadrian's Wall World Heritage Site Partnership

Exhibition loans from:

Archaeological State Collection, Munich, Germany

Archäologisches Landesmuseum Baden-Württemberg / Limes Museum, Aalen, Germany

Laing Art Gallery

Landesmuseum Württemberg, Stuttgart, Germany

Mules of Marius

Markgrafenmuseum, Stadt Ansbach, Germany

Musée d'Art Classique de Mougins (MACM), France

 National Museums Scotland

Province of Lower Austria – Archaeological Park Carnuntum

Society of Antiquaries of Newcastle upon Tyne

Trustees of the British Museum

UK Private Loan

Contributing authors:

Jo Anderson

Barbara Birley

Alexandra Croom

Bill Griffiths

Anne-Marie Knowles

Jane Laskey

Frances McIntosh

Nigel Mills

Tim Padley

Published by: Tyne & Wear Archives & Museums

Publication editor: Georgia Litherland, *in*Heritage

Publication design: Bivouac Ltd

Project management:
Minerva Heritage Ltd
in association with Nigel Mills Heritage

For more information and further reading, visit **hadrianscavalry.co.uk**

HADRIAN'S CAVALRY

For almost 300 years, Roman cavalry troops were stationed along Hadrian's Wall in northern Britain. Explore their world with this beautifully illustrated companion book to the Hadrian's Cavalry exhibition.

Find out where Roman cavalry troops came from, how they trained and how they cared for their horses. Look into their barracks and daily life on the Wall. Discover cavalry rituals and religion. Browse exquisite archaeological finds and learn about the goddess Epona and the Equestrian Games.

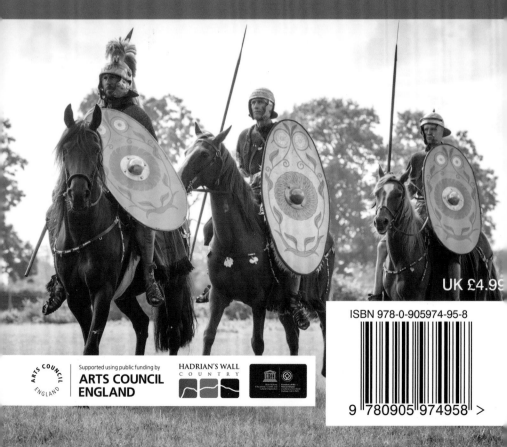

UK £4.99

ISBN 978-0-905974-95-8

9 780905 974958 >

ARTS COUNCIL ENGLAND

Supported using public funding by ARTS COUNCIL ENGLAND

HADRIAN'S WALL COUNTRY